Want to Kno...?

Katy Perry

D0539476

700040807227

PE

WAYLAND

First published in 2013 by Wayland
Copyright © Wayland 2013

Wayland
338 Euston Road
London NW1 3BH

Wayland Australia
Level 17/207 Kent Street
Sydney, NSW 2000

Commissioning editor: Debbie Foy
Series editor: Camilla Lloyd
Designer: Ray Bryant

Dewey categorisation: 782.4'2164'092-dc23

ISBN: 978 0 7502 7931 4

10 9 8 7 6 5 4 3 2 1

Printed in UK
Wayland is a division of Hachette Children's Books,
an Hachette UK company

www.hachette.co.uk

The author and publisher would like to thank the following for allowing
their pictures to be reproduced in this publication: Cover and 25 © Brian
Patterson/Corbis; 4 © Hubert Boesl/dpa/Corbis; 6 © RD/Orchon/Retna
Ltd./Corbis; 14 © Lisa O'Connor/ZUMA Press/Corbis; 30 © Splash News/
Corbis; 51 © Ron Sachs/Corbis; 62 Hubert Boesl/dpa/Corbis; 75 © Britta
Pedersen/dpa/Corbis; 87 © Splash News/Corbis; 89 © UNICEF/Splash
News/Corbis.

This book is not affiliated with or endorsed by Katy Perry.

Want to know
EVERYING
EVERYTHING
there is to
know about

KATY
PERRY?

Then head this way...

KATY PERRY SEEMED
TO SUDDENLY APPEAR, EXPLODING
LIKE A FIREWORK ACROSS THE AIRWAVES – A
RIOT OF OUTRAGEOUS COSTUMES, EVER-CHANGING
HAIRSTYLES AND A POPPY, SASSY ATTITUDE. SHE
WAS THE COMPLETE PACKAGE – GREAT SONGS
AND A UNIQUE LOOK, **BUT**

DO YOU KNOW THE REAL

Katy Perry story?

Here you can discover how Katy made the jump from singing in church to **selling out stadiums**. Full of fascinating facts about Katy's career so far – a **roller coaster ride** of record-breaking successes and also personal lows; the book is packed with **weird** and **wonderful** information.

And if that wasn't enough, on top of all that fun there are **fiendish quizzes** to test your Katy Perry knowledge and torment your brain. Plus there's loads of information on Katy's albums and television appearances (including one that wasn't screened!).

Be shocked at the **danger** she was in on her wedding day! Laugh when you hear what happened when Katy worked with a chimpanzee! Go **awww** when you meet her pets!

WANT TO KNOW YOUR IDOL?

Well turn the page and get your groove on with Katy...

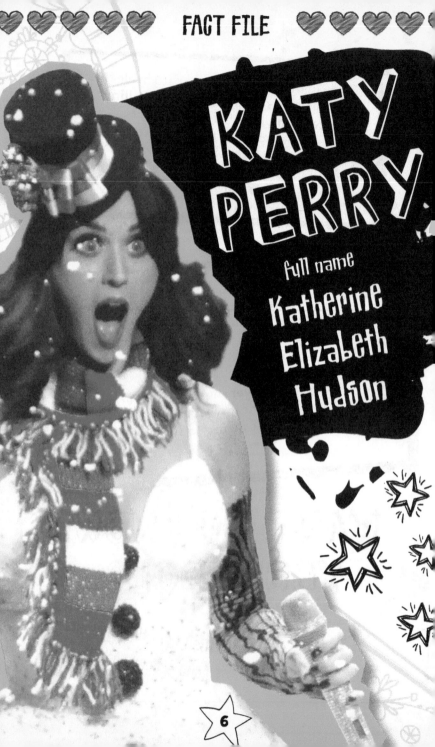

KATY PERRY

full name

Katherine Elizabeth Hudson

Date of birth: 25 October 1984

Place of birth: Santa Barbara, California

Where she lives now: Santa Monica, California

Height: 173 cm (5 feet 7 inches)

Eye colour: Blue-grey

Hair colour: Naturally Katy has strawberry blonde hair

Twitter name: @katyperry

Website: http://www.katyperry.com/

Family

Father: Keith Hudson

Mother: Mary Hudson

Sister: Angela Hudson

Brother: David Hudson

Was anyone less likely to become a pop star than little **Katherine Elizabeth Hudson**? The middle child of Christian ministers Keith and Mary Hudson, Katy had a very **religious** upbringing. She only listened to religious music. Any other kind – including **pop songs** – was banned. Or maybe that was exactly why Katy became a pop star. Maybe she was intrigued by what was forbidden. Either way, no one could have predicted what the future would hold.

What Katy was encouraged to do was to sing. Katy's parents wanted her to sing in the choir at church and even in local restaurants. But the singing had another benefit – her dad paid her **$10 (£7)** every time she sang. Katy realised from an early age she could **make money** by using her talent!

8

So Katy had natural ability, but more importantly, she was also prepared to put the work in. She started having singing lessons when she was nine – turning that raw talent into the voice we know today!

When Katy was 15 her life changed forever. She was at a friend's house and she heard the song **Killer Queen** by the band Queen. Pop music was banned in the Perry household (and in her friends' houses, too) so Katy had never heard anything like it before! It was a total **revelation** – and really, really exciting! If music could sound like that, then Katy wanted to be a part of it!

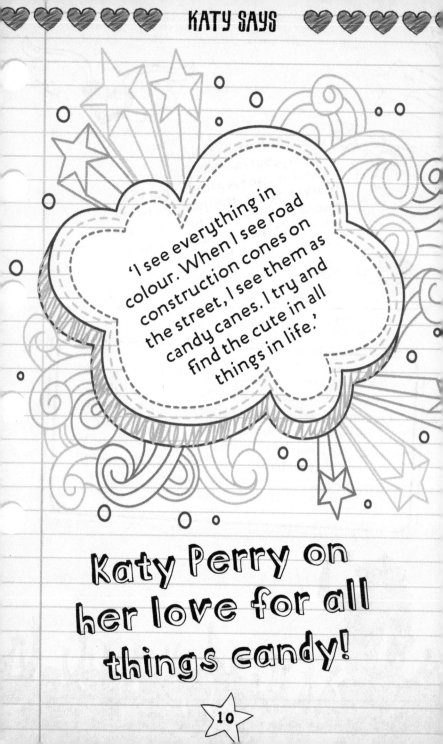

'I see everything in colour. When I see road construction cones on the street, I see them as candy canes. I try and find the cute in all things in life.'

Katy Perry on her love for all things candy!

Katy isn't just a trained singer she also writes her own songs and plays **two musical instruments**. Katy learnt to play the guitar when she was 13 and she also plays the piano. Learning to play an instrument takes time, but Katy knew that **practice makes perfect**, which is why she sounds so good today.

If you can play an instrument it's a big help when writing songs because you can work out the tune as well as the words (known as **lyrics**). Some of the most famous songwriters in music history, write songs on both the guitar and piano, so Katy's in good company!

When Katy was
15 years old she went to
Nashville, Tennessee to learn how
to write songs. Nashville is famous for
being the home of a style of music called
Country and Western. The idea was that Katy
would learn from some of the songwriters
who worked there.

Spending some time
with **professional** songwriters
certainly paid off. She recorded her first
album there – but it was very different from the
kind of album Katy does now. Her first album was
Christian rock – a collection of gospel and religious
songs that Katy had written. Unfortunately
the record label went bust so Katy's first album
was not a success.

Katy moved from Nashville to **Los Angeles** where she worked with a famous record producer called Glen Ballard. He helped improve her songwriting further and got her jobs as a **backing singer** and vocalist and even some album deals. Unfortunately no singles or albums came from the deals and Katy kept getting dropped by the record companies. Money was short and things looked bleak...

Katy kept struggling on and finally her persistence paid off! In 2007 she was signed by **Capitol Music Group**. They realised that Katy knew how to write a hit record and Katy began to have success. Her first two singles **Ur So Gay** and **I Kissed a Girl** made a real splash and the rest is history!

'I kissed God – and I liked it!'

Keith Hudson
adapts one of his daughter's
lyrics for his own sermons.

Katie stands here with (from L-R) her sister,
Dad, Grandmother, Mum and brother.

DAD
Keith

Although Keith is a pastor this isn't always how Katy's dad has lived. In his youth he was a bit of a rebel! He changed his ways when he discovered religion and set up churches. Keith doesn't look like your average preacher; he wears cowboy boots, leather jackets and has a shaved head – perhaps he's still a bit of a rebel!

MUM
Mary

Mary is Katy's mother. Like her husband Keith, she too is a pastor and a committed Christian. Although a lot of Katy's stage shows are not to Mary's taste, mother and daughter are very close and Katy's parents are often at her concerts.

BIG SISTER
Angela

Big sister Angela has always been close to Katy and they spend time together whenever they can. They get on so well that Angela actually worked behind the scenes on Katy's **California Dreams Tour**, meeting and greeting guests.

YOUNGER BROTHER
David

David is the youngest of the Hudson children. Music obviously runs in the family as David is also a singer-songwriter just like his big sis! He has been writing songs since he was 12 years old. In 2013 he released a single from his album.

...that Katy Perry started her recording and music career as **Katy Hudson**?

Katy changed her real name to avoid being confused with the actress **Kate Hudson**.

Although Katy and Kate don't really look alike, the actress is only five years older and came to fame sooner than Katy. It seemed like a good choice to change name – especially as Katy has done film and TV work as well as singing!

And why did Katy choose the surname Perry? It's her **mother's maiden name**!

'I like to go out there looking like a strong woman, because I am strong. But I am also a woman who goes through all kinds of problems and highs and lows.'

She might be a super mega-star but Katy's life has not been all plain sailing. She has the same ups and downs as the rest of us!

The first time doing anything is always special. Here are some of

Katy's firsts:

First boyfriend:
Justin York

First home:
Santa Barbara, California

First album:
Katy Hudson

First pop song she heard: Killer Queen by Queen

First acting role:
A guest appearance in 2011 in the TV series **How I Met Your Mother** playing a character called Honey.

First single:
Trust in Me

... that Katy calls her fans Katycats?

Yep, Katy loves all things cat! They are her favourite animal and she even called one of her tours the **Hello Katy Tour** after the famous Japanese cartoon cat **Hello Kitty!**

Really it was only a matter of time before she came up with the nickname **Katycats** for her fans. The fans love it, of course, it's like being part of a club, and in return they call Katy their **Momma cat.**

We bet she likes that, too!

19

Katy has had an amazing life so far, but can you tell which of these remarkable Katy facts are real and which are made up?!

1 Katy has blue-grey eyes.

2 Katy has massive clown feet and has to have her shoes specially made.

3 Katy once got her head stuck down a manhole.

4 Katy has the third most followers on Twitter in the world.

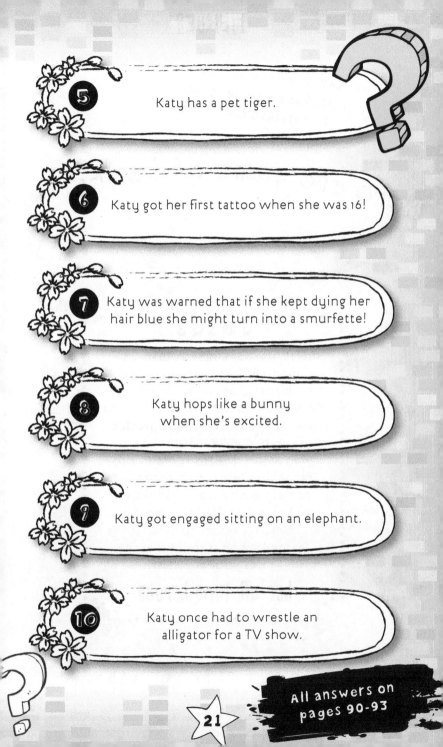

5 Katy has a pet tiger.

6 Katy got her first tattoo when she was 16!

7 Katy was warned that if she kept dying her hair blue she might turn into a smurfette!

8 Katy hops like a bunny when she's excited.

9 Katy got engaged sitting on an elephant.

10 Katy once had to wrestle an alligator for a TV show.

All answers on pages 90-93

21

KATY IS AN INSPIRATION TO HER FANS, BUT WHO HAS INSPIRED KATY?

Here are some of her heroes.

Jesus

He was born in Bethlehem in around 4 BCE and people celebrate his birthday on the 25 December. Christians believe that Jesus was the son of God and **worked miracles** and taught people about the correct way to live. The Islamic faith also recognises Jesus as a prophet and someone who worked miracles. As Katy was raised as a Christian and still believes much of what she learned it's no surprise that she rates Jesus as one of

her all-time heroes.

Ghandi

Peace-loving revolutionary leader, Mohandas 'Mahatma' Gandhi, led the Indian people's struggle against the British rule of India. He was famous for preaching non-violent action, a tactic that eventually paid off. .

Freddie Mercury

His real name was actually Farrokh Bulsara, but he changed his name when the band **Queen** was formed. Queen became one of the world's most successful acts and Freddie was an inspirational and **charismatic** lead singer. He had a wide vocal range, meaning he could hit both very high and very low notes with ease. Most importantly, he was the first non-gospel singer that Katy heard and remained one of her favourite singers of all time.

Angelina Jolie

Although Angelina Jolie is one of the most famous actors alive today it's not her success in the movie business that has made her a hero to Katy, but her tireless work for some of the neediest of the world's citizens. She is a Special Envoy for the **United Nations** and has helped raise the plight of refugees the world over.

HERE'S AN INSIGHT INTO
SOME OF KATY PERRY'S

favourite things:

Place:
Santa Barbara, California

Food:
spaghetti, Thai food,
ice cream

Animal:
cats

Bands/musicians:
Queen, Madonna, Beach Boys,
Freddie Mercury

Colours:
blue and pink

Film:
Blade Runner,
Romeo and Juliet

Sweets:
sour gummy
worms!

Books:
The Help,
The Book of Proverbs

Exercise:
skipping rope

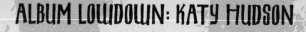

KATY'S FIRST ALBUM WAS ENTITLED **KATY HUDSON** (2001) WHICH IS KATY'S REAL NAME. THE ALBUM WAS MADE UP OF GOSPEL SONGS, BUT SADLY IT DIDN'T SELL – KATY HERSELF RECKONS IT SOLD ABOUT **100 COPIES!** THE GOOD NEWS IS THAT IT FORCED HER TO CHANGE MUSICAL DIRECTION AND THAT'S HOW KATY CAME TO BE THE SINGER WE KNOW TODAY!

RELEASE DATE: 23 OCTOBER 2001

TRACK LIST

1 **TRUST IN ME**
2 **PIERCING**
3 **SEARCH ME**
4 **LAST CALL**
5 **GROWING PAINS**
6 *MY OWN MONSTER*
7 **SPIT**
8 **FAITH WON'T FAIL**
9 **NATURALLY**
10 **WHEN THERE'S NOTHING LEFT**

SINGLES FROM THE ALBUM

1 **TRUST IN ME**
2 **SEARCH ME**

ASTROLOGERS TRY TO PREDICT THE FUTURE BY STUDYING A PERSON'S DATE OF BIRTH AND REFERRING TO THE STARS TO SEE WHAT POSITION THEY WERE IN AT THE TIME.

ASTROLOGERS ALSO BELIEVE THAT YOU CAN TELL A LOT ABOUT A PERSON'S CHARACTER BY THE TIME AND DATE THEY WERE BORN.

ASTROLOGERS SPLIT THE YEAR INTO 12 SEGMENTS NAMED AFTER CONSTELLATIONS. THESE SEGMENTS ARE CALLED THE SIGNS OF THE ZODIAC.

Katy was born on 25 October which according to the zodiac makes her a **Scorpio**. Astrologers say a typical Scorpio is **determined, forceful, energetic and exciting**. However Scorpios can also be jealous, obsessive and obstinate!

Do any of these traits sound like Katy to you?

28

Other famous Scorpios:

Carly Rae Jepsen

Willow Smith

Ryan Gosling

Leonardo Dicaprio

Bill Gates

Prince Charles

Matt Smith (Dr Who)

SOME SCIENTISTS MAY DESCRIBE ASTROLOGY AS BEING A LOAD OF OLD BALONEY – BUT IF YOU DON'T TAKE IT TOO SERIOUSLY THERE'S NO HARM IN IT.

KATY LOVES HER TATTOOS. SHE'S GOT A FEW, BUT THEY'RE ALL SMALL AND DISCREET RATHER THAN BEING HUGE WORKS OF ART. DO YOU KNOW HOW MANY SHE'S GOT – OR MORE IMPORTANTLY, OF WHAT AND WHERE?

1 The word 'Jesus'

Although Katy isn't as strict a Christian as her parents, she still makes time for religion. She's got 'Jesus' tattooed on the inside of her left wrist. She said it is a reminder of her roots and how they are still important to her.

2 Strawberry

Who doesn't love strawberries? Katy certainly does; she's got an inflatable one and has them designed on her stage outfits. She went a stage further than the average strawberry lover though and had one tattooed on her left ankle.

3 Sanskrit writing

Sanskrit is an ancient language and one of the official languages of India. The tattoo Katy has means 'go with the flow' which seems like a good motto for someone with such a hectic life!

4 Peppermint

Candy is a theme in Katy's life and style. So she has a peppermint sweet on her right ankle.

5 Lotus flower

Katy has a small lotus flower tattooed on the inside of her right wrist. Lotus flowers represent purity, beauty and rebirth according to some ancient civilizations.

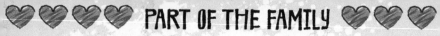
KATY'S STYLE HAS ALWAYS BEEN A BIT CARTOON-LIKE, BUT WE DOUBT SHE THOUGHT SHE'D ACTUALLY END UP IN ONE! BUT IN 2010 KATY WAS INVITED TO GUEST STAR IN **THE SIMPSONS**. THE MEGA-POPULAR TV SHOW HAS BEEN RUNNING SINCE 1989 AND IS THE LONGEST-RUNNING SCRIPTED TV SERIES IN THE WORLD.

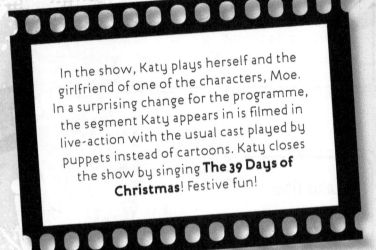

In the show, Katy plays herself and the girlfriend of one of the characters, Moe. In a surprising change for the programme, the segment Katy appears in is filmed in live-action with the usual cast played by puppets instead of cartoons. Katy closes the show by singing **The 39 Days of Christmas**! Festive fun!

Katy joins a galaxy of A-list guest stars who have appeared in The Simpsons.

These amazing names include:

Buzz Aldrin
(astronaut –
second man on
the moon)

Glenn Close
(actor)

Tony Blair
(Prime Minister)

Jeff Goldblum
(actor)

Kirk Douglas
(actor)

Leonard Nimoy
(actor)

U2
(band)

Dolly Parton
(singer)

Elton John
(singer)

Britney Spears
(singer)

Serena Williams
(tennis champion)

Paul Newman
(actor)

Ben Stiller
(actor)

Simon Cowell
(music producer)

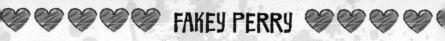

THINK YOU KNOW YOUR KATY PERRY SONGS? WHICH OF THESE ARE FOR REAL AND WHICH ONES ARE NOT SUNG BY

the Queen of Pop?

1. California Gurls
2. Walnut Whip
3. I Kissed a Girl
4. Teenage Dream
5. Old Age Nightmare
6. Thinking of You
7. Hey Jude

8 Firework

9 Peacock

10 Diamonds

11 Fingerprints

12 Wide Awake

13 Boyfriend

14 Ace of Spades

15 Hot N Cold

16 Mild and Humid

17 Part of Me

18 Simple

19 Brain Freeze

20 One of the boys

Which song is your favourite?

35

All answers on pages 90-93

KATY'S BEEN ON BOTH
BIG AND SMALL SCREENS AS A
PERFORMER IN FILMS AND TELEVISION,
BUT NOW KATY PERRY HAS BEEN MADE
INTO A COMPUTER GAME – AND NOT JUST ANY
OLD GAME, BUT A VERSION OF THE SUPER-
SUCCESSFUL **SIMS** SERIES.

Sim City

The Sims has been around since 2004. In the game players control characters, called Sims, in a virtual world. The players controls the Sims' lives from what they buy to where they live. Unlike most PC games there's no prize to aim for, or levels to compete, the idea is to maintain the world that the player has created. **The Sims** is amazingly popular – in fact it's the best-selling PC game **ever!**

Katy's game is called **Sims 3 Katy Perry Sweet Treats**. In it you can dress your Sim in outfits inspired by Katy's wardrobe and the whole environment has been based on a kind of Katy Perry candy-coloured world. Your Sim can even sound like Katy by singing along to a special track Katy recorded just for the game – a unique version of her hit **Last Friday Night**.

Toon-tastic!

'THEY REALLY HAVE COVERED SO MANY OPPORTUNITIES ... YOU COULD BE A DJ, YOU COULD BE A POP STAR ... YOU COULD BE A GYMNAST OR AN ACROBAT. I LOVE THAT YOU GET TO TRY THINGS THAT MAYBE YOU WOULDN'T IN REAL LIFE.'

Katy explains what she likes about playing The Sims

...that
Katy had an
embarrassing
incident with a
chimpanzee during
a photoshoot?

Katy was doing some
modelling work for the
designer Jeremy Scott.
There was a chimpanzee
on the set too (obviously),
and halfway through the
shoot the chimp needed
to go – and urinated on
Katy! Katy had to take a
shower before carrying
on – presumably in some
dry clothes!

'I like to wear things that have a sense of humour and are adorable.'

Well, that describes Katy's wardrobe!

THIS WAS KATY'S FIRST ALBUM UNDER HER NEW NAME AND ITS RELEASE BROUGHT HER TO THE WORLD'S ATTENTION. A NUMBER OF THE TRACKS ON THE ALBUM WERE RELEASED, INCLUDING THE SMASH HITS: I KISSED A GIRL AND HOT N COLD.

Katy Perry was here and we wanted more!

40

ALBUM LOWDOWN: ONE OF THE BOYS

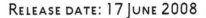

RELEASE DATE: 17 JUNE 2008

TRACK LIST

1   ONE OF THE BOYS
2   I KISSED A GIRL
3   WAKING UP IN VEGAS
4   THINKING OF YOU
5   MANNEQUIN
6   UR SO GAY
7   HOT N COLD
8   IF YOU CAN AFFORD ME
9   LOST
10 SELF INFLICTED
11 I'M STILL BREATHING
12 FINGERPRINTS

SINGLES FROM THE ALBUM

1   I KISSED A GIRL
2   HOT N COLD
3   THINKING OF YOU
4   WAKING UP IN VEGAS

KATY HAS WRITTEN AND
CO-WRITTEN MORE SONGS THAN YOU MIGHT
IMAGINE, BUT EVERY SONG SHE WRITES DOESN'T END
UP AS A SINGLE OR EVEN ON AN ALBUM.

Why?

There are lots of reasons – sometimes they're not 'finished' enough, or Katy doesn't feel they're right for the album. Bad news if you can't get enough of Katy's songs!

The good news though is that even if Katy doesn't want them other people do! Singers **Selena Gomez**, **Kelly Clarkson** and **Jessie James** have all use Katy's songs!

What a talent!

OF COURSE WITH KATY'S BUSY SCHEDULE SHE CAN'T ACTUALLY TO COME ROUND TO YOUR HOUSE, SO WHAT DO YOU DO? HOW ABOUT GETTING A ...

mini me?

No, we don't mean a tiny look-a-like that will sing Katy's songs to you, but a Katy doll that looks just like her!

In 2011, the Katy Perry doll was launched in the USA by Integrity Toys. Only 500 were made though, so getting your hands on one is difficult. Later Mattel (the company that make Barbie) also made a special one-off Katy doll. As it's unique it's even more expensive than the original Katy dolls.

We'd love to see the Katy Perry doll!

YOUR **WEDDING DAY** IS MEANT TO BE ONE OF THE HAPPIEST DAYS OF YOUR LIFE; BUT DURING KATY'S WEDDING TO **RUSSELL BRAND** THEY AND THEIR GUESTS WERE IN DANGER OF BEING **EATEN BY A TIGER**!

Here's the low-down on the story: Katy and Russell tied the knot next door to a tiger sanctuary. Unfortunately, during the time they were there one of the tigers attacked and killed three people. The tiger was still on the loose when the wedding was going on and everyone was worried the wedding celebrations would attract the tiger's attention. Fortunately the tiger was caught just in time!

...that in the early days of Katy's career she was totally broke?

Before Katy hit the big time, life was a real struggle. Her dreams of being a singer were dashed as she was rejected by various record labels. They wanted to make her look and sound like other singers, but Katy wanted to be her own woman.

Fortunately, we know how that story ended up!

IN 2011 KATY BAGGED A
ROLE IN A **BLOCKBUSTER MOVIE** – BUT
FANS ONLY GOT TO HEAR HER VOICE! SHE
WAS PROVIDING THE VOICE FOR **SMURFETTE**,
AN ANIMATED CHARACTER IN THE
MOVIE **THE SMURFS**.

The Smurfs were the creation of a
Belgian artist called Pierre Culliford, but
he called himself Peyo. Culliford loved
tales about trolls and decided to do a
friendlier version, so he came up with
the idea of the Smurfs, funny little blue
creatures that lived inside mushrooms
deep in the forest.

The Smurfs started as a cartoon
strip in 1958, but went on to be
translated into many languages,
TV shows, films and all sorts
of merchandise.

In the film the Smurfs get chased out of their village by the evil wizard Gargamel and end up in the real world, in New York. They have to get back to their village before Gargamel can find them. The movie cleverly combines both animation and real live action, so the Smurfs interact with real life actors.

Smurfette was the very first female Smurf character and was introduced in 1966. She was actually made by the evil wizard Gargamel out of clay to distract the Smurfs, but she soon joined the Smurf community and became a proper Smurf.

The Smurfs was a huge hit – taking over $500 million (£331 million) at the box office!

...that silly string
messed up one of
Katy's concerts?

BACK IN 2008,
KATY WAS DOING A CONCERT
SPONSORED BY A LARGE HAIR PRODUCT
COMPANY. KATY SPENT AN HOUR AND A
HALF GETTING HER HAIR PERFECT TO ADVERTISE
THE HAIR PRODUCTS BEFORE SHE WENT ON STAGE.
UNFORTUNATELY AS THE CONCERT STARTED SHE
WENT TO SHOOT SOME SILLY STRING INTO THE
CROWD – BUT HAD THE CAN THE WRONG WAY
ROUND! INSTEAD OF SPRAYING THE
CROWD SHE SPRAYED HER OWN
LOVELY HAIRDO!

Katy suffers from obsessive compulsive disorder. When she gets severe bouts of OCD it can lead to panic attacks. But what is it that triggers Katy's OCD?

Actually it's things that make her messy such as finger marks on sunglasses or even cat hair on her clothes.

Katy isn't the only famous person to suffer from OCD. For example international football star David Beckham has the condition, too.

People with OCD can be helped in lots of different ways, depending on how severe the condition is. Often it's a case of learning how to control the way they think about things. As Katy still has her pet cats she must be doing well and working hard at living with OCD.

THINK YOU KNOW KATY'S SONGS? THINK AGAIN!
TRY THIS TEST OF YOUR KP KNOWLEDGE WITH OUR
ANAGRAM TEASER. EACH OF THESE 12 SONG TITLES
HAS BEEN REARRANGED – CAN YOU WORK OUT
WHAT THEY ARE?

ENTRY LEVEL

T.E.

SLOT

PALER

PITS

GETTING HARDER

RIFER WOK

CAKE COP

TALL AY RUN

DEGENERATE AM

KATYCATS ONLY

A FROLIC SINGULAR

HOT HOT NEAT GATEWAY

ODOUR IF FANCY FAME

WIN PUKE SAVAGING

All answers on
pages 90-93

'Ever since I was younger I wanted to be on stage, singing my songs in a glittering costume. And that happened and is still happening.'

...that Katy was a first in the US charts?

IN 2011-12 KATY BECAME THE FIRST FEMALE SOLO ARTIST TO HAVE FIVE NUMBER ONE SINGLES FROM THE SAME ALBUM.

Way to go Katy!

Bonus quiz

DO YOU KNOW WHAT THOSE FIVE SINGLES WERE?

53

All answers on pages 90-93

WE'VE ALREADY DISCOVERED THAT KATY PACKS A STING AS A **SCORPIO** (WELL ACCORDING TO THE ZODIAC ANYWAY – SEE PAGES 28-29); BUT WHAT ABOUT OTHER TYPES OF ASTROLOGY? THE CHINESE NAME EACH YEAR AFTER AN ANIMAL. THERE ARE 12 ANIMALS WHICH THEY USE IN A CYCLE – A BIT LIKE THE SIGNS OF THE ZODIAC.

As Katy was born in 1984, that would make her a **rat**. Not the most appealing animal we're sure that you'll agree. But is it all bad news? Nope. In fact the good news is that the sign of the rat is **pretty cool**!

PEOPLE BORN IN THE YEAR OF THE RAT ARE SAID TO BE:

courageous, energetic, charismatic, hard-working, and popular

Yay!

(They're also said to be a bit stubborn but let's ignore that bit...)

OTHER FAMOUS PEOPLE BORN IN THE YEAR OF THE RAT INCLUDE:

WILLIAM SHAKESPEARE

CAMERON DIAZ

SCARLETT JOHANSSON

PRINCE CHARLES

GEORGE WASHINGTON

MONET

MARLON BRANDO

GALILEO

MOZART

55

KATY'S THIRD ALBUM WAS A BIT MORE RELAXED THAN HER PREVIOUS ONES. BEING AN **ACOUSTIC** ALBUM MEANT THERE WERE NO ELECTRONIC INSTRUMENTS WHICH GAVE MORE FOCUS TO KATY'S **FABULOUS VOICE**. IT'S ALSO HER FIRST LIVE ALBUM, RECORDED IN FRONT OF AN AUDIENCE OF LUCKY FANS.

The album also came with a DVD of the concert and a Katy interview. We think you will agree that it's ...

...a must for all fans!

Release date: 17 June 2008

Track list

1. I KISSED A GIRL
2. UR SO GAY
3. HACKENSACK
4. THINKING OF YOU
5. LOST
6. WAKING UP IN VEGAS
7. BRICK BY BRICK

When Katy played at the **MTV Video Music Awards** in 2009 she was expecting a great show, but she actually got more than that – she met her future husband! The British comedian and actor, **Russell Brand**, was hosting the show and was clearly quite taken with Katy. He made references during the show about her and by the end of the night they were chatting like old friends!

Who would have guessed what that meeting would lead to? The pair found they got on **fantastically** well. One night in England the two were sharing a curry and Katy mentioned how much she loved all things Indian. Shortly afterwards romantic Russell surprised her with a **trip to India**!

When Katy tweeted a picture of herself at the **Taj Mahal**, few people could have known what was to happen next. The famous Indian landmark is said to be one of the most **romantic places on Earth**, so maybe something rubbed off – a few days later at the exclusive Taj Rambagh Palace Hotel in Jaipur, India, Russell **proposed** to Katy. And she said

YES!

People used to seeing Katy's **wild stage clothes** or Russell's usual scruffy look might have been surprised by how classic and simple the engagement ring was. It was a single three-carat **diamond ring** designed by Cartier.

KATY MAY HAVE HAD
ONE OF THE BIG **CELEBRITY**
WEDDINGS OF THE YEAR, BUT WHEN
SHE MARRIED RUSSELL BRAND IN 2010
THE NUPTIALS WERE CONDUCTED IN
PRIVATE WITH JUST FRIENDS AND FAMILY
AND **NO PAPARAZZI** WERE INVITED.
SOMETIMES EVEN **BIG STARS** LIKE
KATY DON'T WANT TO SHINE
ALL THE TIME.

The privacy that Katy and
Russell enjoyed when they
got engaged obviously
meant a lot to them.
When they got married
they held the ceremony
in the grounds of the very
exclusive Aman-i-Khás
hotel in India. Russell
Brand was reported to have
presented his bride with
a Bengal tiger as a token of
his love for her!

Any event where Katy is involved isn't going to be run of the mill. Even though her wedding was very private it was still spectacular! Reports suggest that there was **a parade of elephants** – how cool is that? And they weren't the only animals to attend either – there were also **camels** and **horses**!

Although Russell isn't religious and they were getting married in India (a mainly Hindu country) the happy couple were still married by a Christian minister.

According to reports about the wedding, Katy's dress was a dove grey creation from the designer Elie Saab's haute couture range. Katy's shoes were unique beaded satin heels, reportedly worth **$7000 (£4,500)!**

No one likes a party more than Katy and Russell

and the next day they had a big bash to celebrate their wedding. They held the wedding party at the same hotel as the one they got engaged in — the swanky Taj Rambagh Palace Hotel in Jaipur.

AFTER THE WEDDING KATY AND RUSSELL WENT ON HONEYMOON TO THE MALDIVE ISLANDS. THERE ARE OVER A THOUSAND OF THESE BEAUTIFUL ISLANDS SCATTERED IN TWO CLUMPS IN THE INDIAN OCEAN AND THEY ARE POPULAR WITH HONEYMOONERS AND SCUBA DIVERS.

After relaxing there they went to Thailand for a holiday, too!

KATY REALLY HIT THE BIG TIME WITH THE ALBUM **TEENAGE DREAM**. THE ALBUM WENT TO NUMBER 1 IN LOADS OF COUNTRIES INCLUDING THE UK AND USA – AND THERE WERE A STAGGERING SIX SINGLES RELEASED FROM THE ALBUM. THE SINGLES WERE SUPER-SUCCESSFUL TOO, WITH MEGA-HITS LIKE **FIREWORK** AND **CALIFORNIA GURLS** TOPPING CHARTS AROUND THE WORLD.

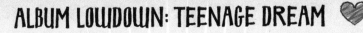

RELEASE DATE: 24 AUGUST 2010

TRACK LIST

1 **TEENAGE DREAM**
2 **LAST FRIDAY NIGHT** (T.G.I.F)
3 **CALIFORNIA GURLS**
   (FEATURING SNOOP DOGG)
4 **FIREWORK**
5 **PEACOCK**
6 **CIRCLE THE DRAIN**
7 **THE ONE THAT GOT AWAY**
8 **E.T.**
9 **WHO AM I LIVING FOR?**
10 **PEARL**
11 **HUMMINGBIRD HEART**
12 **NOT LIKE THE MOVIES**

SINGLES FROM THE ALBUM

1 **CALIFORNIA GURLS**
2 **TEENAGE DREAM**
3 **FIREWORK**
4 **E.T.**
5 **LAST FRIDAY NIGHT** (T.G.I.F)
6 **THE ONE THAT GOT AWAY**

WITHOUT DOUBT, KATY THINKS
THAT CATS MAKE THE

purrfect pets!

SHE'S CRAZY ABOUT CATS AND DOESN'T LIKE
BEING AWAY FROM HER

marvellous moggies!

HER MOST FAMOUS CAT IS THE
GRANDLY NAMED **KITTY PURRY** –

how cute is that?

KITTY PURRY IS NO STRANGER TO THE
LIMELIGHT. KATY OFTEN TWEETS PICTURES OF
KITTY AND FANS CAN ALSO CATCH A GLIMPSE
OF THE FABULOUS FELINE IN THE VIDEO FOR
KATY'S SONG **I KISSED A GIRL**. KATY HAS
THREE OTHER CATS APART FROM KITTY, TOO:

Krusty, Monkey and Morrisey

THE SERIOUS BIT

CATS HAVE BEEN SPECIAL COMPANIONS FOR PEOPLE FOR THOUSANDS OF YEARS. CATS WERE KEPT AS PETS AS LONG AGO AS THE ANCIENT EGYPTIAN TIMES – PARTICULARLY PRIZED MOGGIES WERE EVEN MUMMIFIED WHEN THEY DIED! OF COURSE CATS ARE ESPECIALLY USEFUL FOR CATCHING MICE; A TALENT THAT SAW THEM TAKEN TO SEA ABOARD OCEAN-GOING SHIPS!

Can you work out who's being described here?

Give yourself:

4 points

IF YOU GET THE ANSWER ON THE FIRST CLUE,

3 points

IF YOU GET IT ON THE SECOND,

2 points

ON THE THIRD

AND

1 point

IF YOU GET IT ON THE LAST.

1. I AM ONE OF KATY'S HEROES.
2. I INSPIRED HER TO SING.
3. ONE OF MY SONGS WAS THE FIRST POP RECORD SHE EVER HEARD.
4. I WAS IN THE BAND QUEEN.

1. I'M VERY CLOSE TO KATY.
2. I HAVE APPEARED IN A KATY PERRY VIDEO.
3. I SOUND A BIT LIKE KATY PERRY.
4. I'M A CAT.

1. I LIKE WEARING BLACK.
2. I'M AN ACTOR.
3. THOUGH I MIGHT BE BETTER KNOWN AS A COMEDIAN.
4. I WAS MARRIED TO KATY.

1. I GREW UP IN SANTA BARBARA.
2. I KNOW KATY BETTER THAN MOST PEOPLE.
3. I'M YOUNGER THAN KATY.
4. MY STAGE NAME IS HUDSON.

How did you get on?

69

All answers on pages 90-93

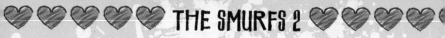

As the 2011 movie **The Smurfs** was such a massive hit, it was only a matter of time before a sequel was made. In 2013 **The Smurfs 2** was released – complete with Katy voicing the part of Smurfette again!

In the film, the evil wizard Gargamel has created the Naughties – and as their name suggests they're up to no good. Fortunately for the Smurfs, Smurfette knows how to solve the problem. Unfortunately for Smurfette, this knowledge gets her kidnapped as Gargamel tries to stop his evil plans from being thwarted.

As you might expect, many of the stars of the first film are back with a couple of new additions for good measure. Katy is joined by superstar names like Christina Ricci, Alan Cumming and Brendan Gleeson.

Rumour has it that the work started on the script for this film just a couple of weeks after the first film was released. The studio must have realised quite early on that the film was going to be a success - and they were right!

UNFORTUNATELY KATY'S
MARRIAGE TO RUSSELL BRAND
DID NOT LAST. ON 30 DECEMBER 2011,
RUSSELL CONFIRMED THE RUMOURS THAT HAD
BEEN CIRCULATING WHEN HE TWEETED:

> 'Sadly, Katy and I are ending our marriage. I'll always adore her and I know we'll remain friends.'

Apparently Katy and Russell had
been having difficulties for some
time and hadn't spent Christmas
together. Breaking up is hard for any
couple, but when you do it under
the glare of the world's press then
it becomes very difficult indeed.
However, Katy also felt huge
support from her fans and took to
Twitter to say:

> 'I am so grateful for all the love and support I've had from people around the world.'

In 2012 things seemed to be looking up for Katy as she started dating the singer **John Mayer**. Katy and the Grammy Award-winning singer went public with their relationship in late 2012 and for a while everything was looking good. But it was not to last.

Rumours of problems between the two began to do the rounds and in the spring of 2013 Katy and John split up.

LOOKING GOOD IS IMPORTANT WHEN YOU'RE A
GLOBAL MEGASTAR – AND SO IS KEEPING YOUR LOOK
FRESH. WE ALL LOVE KATY'S **OUTRAGEOUS OUTFITS**,
BUT THEY JUST WOULDN'T BE COMPLETE WITHOUT HER
EVER-CHANGING HAIR! KATY'S HAD MORE HAIRSTYLES
AND COLOURS THAN SOME BANDS HAVE HAD HIT
RECORDS. SOME OF HER HAIRSTYLES HAVE BEEN:

long, short, bobbed, curled
side-parted, fringed,
and
soft rolled.

ADD TO THAT THE COLOURS:

red, blue, purple,
ginger, blonde,
AND OF COURSE:
black!

Which colour and style
was your favourite?

'I REALLY LIKE TO LOOK LIKE A HISTORY BOOK. I CAN LOOK 1940s, I CAN LOOK 1970s HIPPY-CHIC, OR SOMETIMES I'LL PULL THAT '80s BROOKLYN HIP-HOP KID WITH THE DOOR-KNOCKER EARRINGS.'

No danger of Katy getting stuck in a rut about what to wear or how to style her hair! How big must her wardrobe be?

GLOBAL SUPERSTARS LIKE KATY SPEND A LOT OF THEIR TIME ON THE ROAD ON TOUR. THE GOOD SIDE OF THIS IS YOU GET TO TRAVEL TO CITIES AND COUNTRIES YOU'VE NEVER BEEN TO BEFORE. THE DOWNSIDE IS THAT YOU RARELY GET TO SPEND LONG ENOUGH THERE TO SEE ANYTHING!

So far Katy's been to:

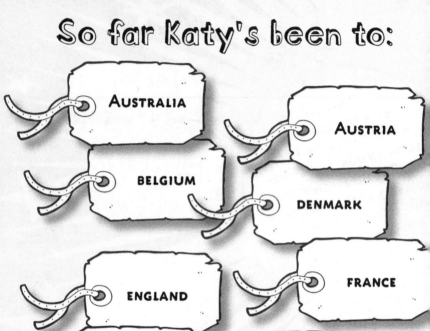

AUSTRALIA

AUSTRIA

BELGIUM

DENMARK

ENGLAND

FRANCE

GERMANY

IRELAND

ITALY

JAPAN

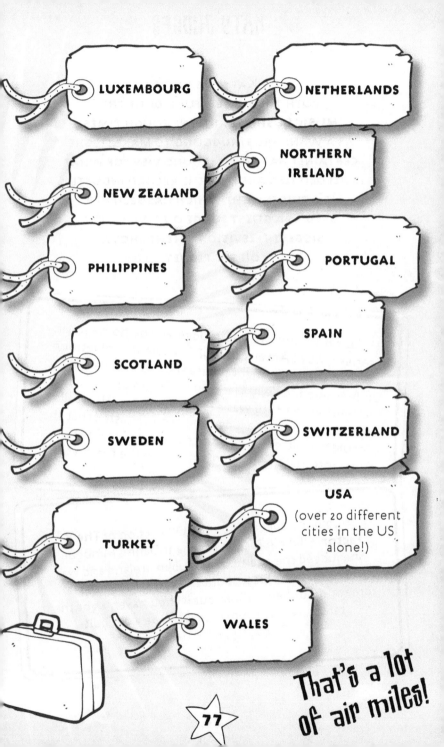

LUXEMBOURG

NETHERLANDS

NORTHERN IRELAND

NEW ZEALAND

PHILIPPINES

PORTUGAL

SPAIN

SCOTLAND

SWEDEN

SWITZERLAND

USA
(over 20 different cities in the US alone!)

TURKEY

WALES

That's a lot of air miles!

As KATY HAS KNOWN
BOTH THE SUCCESSFUL SIDE OF THE
MUSIC BUSINESS AND THE TOUGH TIMES
AS A WANNABE STRUGGLING TO MAKE IT, SHE
CERTAINLY HAS AN ALL-ROUND VIEW OF WHAT
IS NEEDED TO MAKE IT IN THE RECORD INDUSTRY.
IT'S THIS INSIGHT WHICH HAS SEEN HER
USED AS A **GUEST JUDGE** ON TWO OF THE
BIGGEST TELEVISION TALENT SHOWS
ON THE PLANET.

Katy's first stint as a guest judge was on home soil in series nine of **American Idol**. The talent competition had already brought future stars such as Carrie Underwood and Kelly Clarkson to the American public's attention and Katy was a fan of the show. She really enjoyed her time as a judge and even admitted that she could happily give up her career and do judging full-time! Fortunately she didn't give in to the temptation.

In 2010 she appeared on the UK version of **The X Factor**, filling in for the pregnant Dannii Minogue. She judged the auditions in Dublin, Ireland and was very matter of fact about the acts. Many people dream about being a star, but if they haven't got the talent, telling them nicely can be a difficult. Of course, Katy nailed it!

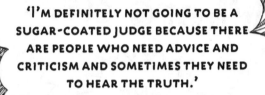

'I'M DEFINITELY NOT GOING TO BE A SUGAR-COATED JUDGE BECAUSE THERE ARE PEOPLE WHO NEED ADVICE AND CRITICISM AND SOMETIMES THEY NEED TO HEAR THE TRUTH.'

'I'VE ONLY BEEN IN THE INDUSTRY ... FOR ABOUT TWO OR THREE YEARS, BUT I'VE BEEN WORKING AT IT A LONG TIME AND I KNOW WHAT IT TAKES TO MAKE IT.'

♡♡♡ THE MEGA KATY PERRY QUIZ ♡♡

YOU'VE READ THE BOOK, NOW DO YOU
HAVE THE KNOWLEDGE? HERE ARE
SOME BRAIN-TEASERS TO TEST AND
TORMENT EVEN THE SAVVIEST KATYCAT.
HOW WELL WILL YOU DO?

where did...

1. KATY GROW UP?

2. KATY LEARN ABOUT THE RECORD BUSINESS?

3. KATY GO ON HONEYMOON?

Who...

4. INSPIRED KATY WITH THEIR SONG **KILLER QUEEN**?

5. DID KATY PLAY IN **THE SMURFS**?

6. IS KATY'S SISTER?

7. IS THE ACTRESS WHOSE NAME WAS VERY CLOSE TO KATY'S?

What...

8. Is Katy's brother's stage name?

9. Exotic animal did Katy get as a wedding present?

10. Award did Katy get in November 2012?

11. Record label did Katy sign to in 2007?

12. What is Katy's Chinese Zodiac animal?

13. Is the name of her second perfume?

14. Are Katy's favourite foods?

15. Does Katy have tattooed on her right and left ankles?

True or False

3. KATY HAS AN ELEPHANT TATTOO

2. KATY HAD FOUR US NUMBER 1s IN 2012

1. KATY HAS A CAT CALLED KITTY FURRY

5. KATY HAS PERFORMED IN OVER 20 DIFFERENT COUNTRIES

4. KATY'S DAD USED TO PAY HER TO SING

8. KATY LOVES CANDY COLOURS!

6. KATY HAD AN UNFORTUNATE INCIDENT WITH A CHIMPANZEE

7. KATY LOVES SKIPPING

10. KATY CAN CHANGE THE COLOUR OF HER HAIR JUST BY THINKING ABOUT IT REALLY, REALLY HARD

9. KATY'S FAVOURITE CHILDHOOD PASTTIME WAS LISTENING TO POP SONGS

Random

2. **RUYCR** IS AN ANAGRAM OF THE MEAL KATY AND RUSSELL WERE EATING WHEN SHE TALKED ABOUT INDIA

1. NAME KATY'S FOUR ALBUMS

4. WHAT IS KATY'S MIDDLE NAME?

3. WHO SANG ON CALIFORNIA GURLS WITH KATY?

6. WHAT DOES KATY'S MOTHER DO FOR HER JOB?

5. WHAT IS HER DATE OF BIRTH?

8. WHAT WAS KATY'S FIRST TATTOO?

7. WHAT WAS THE NAME OF THE TV CARTOON SERIES KATY APPEARED IN?

All answers on pages 90-93

SESAME STREET IS ONE OF THE MOST FAMOUS TELEVISION PROGRAMMES ON AMERICAN TELEVISION AND IS SHOWN AROUND THE WORLD. THE CHILDREN'S SHOW HAS BEEN RUNNING SINCE 1969 AND FEATURES PUPPETS CREATED BY JIM HENSON – OR **MUPPETS** AS THEY ARE KNOWN. MANY OF THESE MUPPETS, SUCH AS **BIG BIRD, ELMO, OSCAR THE GROUCH, ERNIE** AND **COUNT VON COUNT** ARE STARS IN THEIR OWN RIGHT!

When Katy was younger she would have known all about this educational children's television show. So you can imagine how thrilled she would have been when she was asked to appear as a guest star!

Katy was meant to sing a version of **Hot N Cold** to the character Elmo who can't make up his mind whether he wants to play or not. The segment is really good fun and Katy shows all of her comic acting talents.

When people saw the preview clips there was uproar. Many people thought that Katy's dress was too revealing for a children's show. In the end Katy's song was cut from the show. Of course, her clothes were quite tame compared to some of the wilder creations she wears on stage, but the decision had been made for a good reason.

What are your thoughts on Katy's style?

What do you do once you've already got **BEST-SELLING RECORDS** and **SELL-OUT TOURS** under your belt? Make a perfume that's what! She released her first scent in 2010 and called it **PURR**, of course! The citrus-based scent was even packaged in a purple cat-shaped bottle to match its name.

'IT'S A GORGEOUS BLEND OF ALL MY FAVOURITE SCENTS THAT EMBODIES MY STYLE, MY TASTES AND MY LOVE FOR ALL THINGS INCREDIBLY CUTE.'

Katy

With sales of **Purr** going well, Katy developed her second scent. Continuing the cat theme, Katy called this perfume **Meow**! And it was packaged in a pink cat-shape bottle like before. Work on the perfume began while Katy was on tour. She wanted a smell that captured the fun and excitement of performing live. As opposed to the nervous sweat and fast food smells that sometimes hang around concert venues!

'WE HAVE A LOT OF FUN ON TOUR SO THERE'S A LOT OF FUN INFUSED INSIDE THIS BOTTLE!'

Katy

EVEN KATY ADMITS THAT
2012 WAS A ROLLER COASTER OF A
YEAR. THERE WERE HIGHS AND LOWS, BUT
AMIDST IT ALL THERE WAS AN AMAZING PIECE
OF NEWS – ON 30 NOVEMBER KATY WAS
NAMED BILLBOARD'S

Woman of the Year!

Billboard is the organisation that monitors American record sales. Originally it started life as a magazine for the record industry, but now is best known for the **Billboard Hot 100 singles chart** and the **Billboard 200 album chart**. These are charts that give the official Number 1 singles and albums.

Part of the reason Katy got the award was for the amazing sales she had in 2012. She sold around 48 million songs just in the USA and had a record five number 1s on the **Hot 100 chart**. On top of that she sold out 124 concert venues. Pretty impressive stats!

The other (even more important) reason Katy got the award was for the work she did for charity. That year she raised money for charities including the **Red Cross** and the **Humane Society**. It's good to give something back when you've had success!

'KATY PERRY IS HANDS-DOWN ONE OF THE MOST EXCITING AND INSPIRING ARTISTS IN THE INDUSTRY TODAY.'

Bill Werde, Editorial Director of **Billboard**

We couldn't agree more!

PAGES 20-21
TRUE OR FALSE?

1. TRUE
2. FALSE
3. FALSE
4. TRUE – ONLY LADY GAGA AND
JUSTIN BIEBER HAVE MORE
5. TRUE
6. TRUE
7. FALSE
8. TRUE
9. TRUE
10. FALSE

PAGES 34-35
FAKEY PERRY

THEY ARE ALL KATY'S SONGS
APART FROM NUMBERS

2
5
7
13
14 AND
19

PAGES 50
IN A MUDDLE

ENTRY LEVEL

E.T.
LOST
PEARL
SPIT

GETTING HARDER

FIREWORK
PEACOCK
NATURALLY
TEENAGE DREAM

KATYCATS ONLY

CALIFORNIA GURLS
THE ONE THAT GOT AWAY
IF YOU CAN AFFORD ME
WAKING UP IN VEGAS

PAGE 53
BONUS QUIZ

THE SINGLES WERE:
CALIFORNIA GURLS, TEENAGE DREAM,
FIREWORK, E.T., LAST FRIDAY NIGHT (T.G.I.F.)

Pages 68-69
Guess Who?

Freddie Mercury
Kitty Purry
Russell Brand
David Hudson

Pages 80-81
Mega Katy Perry Quiz

Where did...?

1. Santa Barbara, California
2. Nashville, Tennessee
3. The Maldives

Who...?

4. Queen
5. Smurfette
6. Angela Hudson
7. Kate Hudson

What...?

8. Hudson
9. A tiger
10. Billboard Woman of the Year
11. Capitol Music Group
12. A rat
13. Meow!

14. Spaghetti and Thai food
15. She has a peppermint on her right
and a strawberry on her left

Page 82
True or False

1. False – it's Kitty Purry
2. False – she had 5!
3. False
4. True
5. True
6. True
7. True
8. False
9. False – she wasn't allowed to
10. False!

Page 83
Random

1. Katy Hudson, One of the Boys,
MTV Unplugged, Teenage Dream
2. Curry
3. Snoop Dogg
4. Elizabeth
5. 25 October 1984
6. Pastor
7. The Simpsons
8. The word 'Jesus'

 # INDEX

Congratulations!

Now you really, truly **KNOW** your idol
(probably better than her own mum).
But what about your **OTHER** idols, like
One Direction, **Olly Murs**, **Robert
Pattinson** and **James Arthur?**

WHAT ABOUT THEM...?

DON'T PANIC.

Simply check out the other titles
in the series and become an

EVEN
BIGGER
FAN.

Want to Know Your Idol?

TOTALLY AWESOME TITLES IN THE SERIES:

9780750279321

9780750279338

9780750279307

9780750279314

9780750278386

9780750278362

WHY NOT COLLECT THEM ALL?